WORKSHOP #1

ELECTRONIC TRADE DOCUMENTATION

BY
RITA CONTE

SYNERGENICS CONSULTING
Delivering Solutions

Table of Contents

Introduction

While there is clear evidence of the use of a document like the bill of lading in Roman times, for the purposes of the use of the ocean bill of lading, it may be said that the modern bill of lading was born in the Eleventh Century, which marked the rise of the great commercial cities of the Mediterranean. In its original creation, the Ocean Bill of Lading, as a trade document, identifies the possession of ownership of goods through a paper form as it is carried out for commercial use, customs, and possession.

Today, technology under an electronic trade document has altered the use and transferability of an original paper to have the same legal relevance as an original signed copy. Evaluating the definition of a paper bill of lading and its importance in the transition to electronic trade documentation is the key takeaway from this book, providing those in the business of ship financing, trade agreements with insight into how trade and shipping will look in the future.

We examine the impacts, effects, and transition of implementing internationally a standard electronic trade documentation system. We examine the processes and resources required to ensure a system of reliability, efficiency in place of a traditional paper document. What needs to be enforced is equal accessibility, creative competition, and standards by each jurisdiction, which are realistic to the cost of the infrastructure and funding by governments.

This is an introduction to simplify the processes, while taking an analytical approach to examine both systems of documentation in both their forms, recommended by industry and adopted by each country or state under laws and statutes, as we see with the UK Act of 2023.

The objective is to understand why a new system is put in place in terms of the vision of the world's global elitists in advancing technology through controls, surveillance, and uniformity that creates a one-world system of how trade is managed in record keeping. What does this mean for the companies and small to mid-size enterprises that trade goods across major nations with a limited amount of capital and manpower in staying in business, and who are the drivers from the top of the investment pole pushing for changes of this scope? Both systems need to ensure reliability, legal force, and legislative approvals, efficiency, flexibility, and equal access to market share and trading opportunities of all players in the system of maritime trade, regardless of volumes, destination, or capital and human resources. Competition is key to a healthy trading environment, assuring maritime nations that have the subsidies and central government support monetarily are not imposing laws that limit access to market share for smaller nations, carriers, or cargo owners.

1.1 The Definition Of The Paper Bill Of Lading

The definition of a paper trade document is that it is in paper form, used in at least one part of the United Kingdom, and is connected through trade and transport of goods, including financing such trade and transport, requiring possession of the document as a matter of law, or commercial customs, practices, or usage.[1]

What makes the bill so different from others, specifically the bill of exchange, a promissory note, a ship's delivery order, a warehouse receipt, a marine insurance policy, a cargo insurance certificate, is its physical properties and function. The document itself attaches transfer rights or obligations through its ownership it possesses in releasing or transferring title to another party, specifically the buyer or consignee named on the bill of lading itself. The importance of the exchange between the carrier and consignee or notify party is the obligation of payment by the bearer in the sum of money or delivery of goods when they are in possession of this instrument.[2]

Being the holder of the possession of the Original Bill of Lading has significance in its ability to be recognized as a tangible document that does not need to be elevated in its legal authenticity because it is not an electronic form that is intangible. When a letter of credit is issued through a representing bank overseas and in the seller's own jurisdiction, the terms and conditions of the letter of credit provide the rules and regulations specific to the acceptance of the Ocean Bill of Lading. The original Bill of Lading in its original signed form, not the copy, acts as a receipt of transfer confirming the release of goods upon delivery. The possessor of the bill assures transfer of goods to the consignee named on the original bill of lading as a carrier of the goods while in transit over water to meet its next transfer point of delivery on land.

2.1 The UK Electronic Trade Documents Act 2023

The UK Electronic Act aims to give electronic documents the same legal status as paper ones, ensuring that the Carriage of Goods Act remains legally valid in maritime exchanges of bills of lading, with clauses supporting ETDA transferability. In other words, the ETDA will give equal legal equivalence to the electronic form as the paper form in its legal recognition as their paper counterparts only if it is reliable. The ETDA electronic system cannot legally substitute or compromise existing legal systems, as it needs to be preserved.[3]

The Act attempts to transform an intangible trade document in electronic form into an asset that can be possessed, providing it with the same legal usage and recognition as a paper copy. The criteria that would be required under an electronic document form, specifically in reference to an Ocean Bill of Lading that holds title.

---

[1] Electronic Trade Documents Act 2023, chapter 38, (UK).
[2] Electronic Trade Documents Act 2023, chapter 38, (UK).
[3] Clifford Chance, UK Electronic Trade Documents Act 2023: A Further Step Towards Paperless Trade. www.cliffordchance.com.

The right to titleship and ownership of goods is its reliability to carry out its obligation of performance while in one's possession. All information and data associated with the electronic form in its full purpose under the UK Act is a reliable system when used for specific purposes.

For example, the following are good examples of specific functions the UK Act is required to uphold in assuring the reliability of an Ocean Bill of Lading in its electronic form.

a. Identify the document so it can be distinguished from any other document

b. Protect the document against unauthorized alterations.

c. Secure that it is not possible for more than one person to exercise control of the document at any one time.

d. Allow any person who can exercise control of the document to demonstrate that the person is able to do so.

e. Secure that a transfer of the document has the effect to deprive any person who was able to exercise control of the document immediately before the transfer of the ability to do so (unless the person can exercise control by virtue of being a transferee).[4]

The transferability from one document to the other in either form would require the electronic document to be standardized to meet specific criteria that would not undermine its use as a legal instrument, specifically if a legal dispute would arise and the documents would be required in the courts to defend either party. The case law provided as part of this analysis provides a good example of how the original bill is used to withhold cargo by the carrier to ensure payment is secured by the shipper in case they default, being in breach of Charter Party terms. The bill is used as a powerful possession of financial collateral in securing hire payments between the carrier and shipper, holding no third-party influence in how this relationship is defined in its delivery obligations. In this case, a dispute arose between the carrier and the cargo owner due to bills of lading released against the authority of the captain by the representing agent when a "letter of authorization" was issued by the captain of the vessel MV Padre. The reasoning behind the letter of authorization in the assurance of the bill of lading being held and not released to the named consignee or the cargo owner's representative was based on securing payment in the event the shipper would default on payment for transportation services under the Charter Party Agreement.

The use of an electronic bill of lading in disputes arising under the above circumstances between the carrier and the cargo owner may not hold legal weight in a court of law or be recognized as a legal document as submissible evidence in a legal dispute in a foreign jurisdiction. The seamless transfer of an electronic bill of lading needs to stand the test of law in its legal form, regardless of how efficient, seamless, or effective the transfer of data may be in securing large amounts of financing under a digital system. Tracking and tracing events surrounding the bill of lading historical data or possession also plays a valid factor of concern when deciding to implement a system such as this. The case presented for the electronic form entails the delivery to be seamless, without delay or disruptions as release of goods at the destination specified on the bill of lading, in which it has not been put to the test or in use during times of disasters, force majeure, labor stoppages or global disruptions to shipments due to war, pandemics or

---

[4] Electronic Trade Documentation Act 2023, Chapter 38, (UK).

conflicts. The obligation rests on the well-defined distinction between a legal electronic form and a paper form, each having to hold its own terms of agreement and conditions that provide legal rights, to the ownership of the cargo and its delivery. Both the UK Act and the Scottish Act, under legal recognition of the electronic trade document, see it as a movable property that serves the purpose relating to creating a security in the form of a pledge over movable property.[5]

3.1 New Technology, Supporting Platforms, And Compatibility

Today, a commonly used technology such as DCSA is used under trade initiatives for the purpose of facilitating acceptance and adoption of electronically transmitted documents to strengthen the process of transferring the bill of lading, using the digital speed of paperless and seamless transactions. What drives this intense push to transform an existing world of trade documentation into a swift, high-speed digital system is the projected increase in trade revenues in the millions, discounting the fact that the financial shipping market is highly saturated. In other words, the volume of trades originated through trade agreements between buyer and seller is reflective of global market conditions of supply and demand, including consumer confidence in manufactured goods. The ability to replace a required signed document, such as a bill of lading, with a transferable receipt on the other side of the world requires checks in place to ensure that the strict authorization of release of cargo against a mate's receipt is not compromised.

The financial obligation on the part of the charterer still needs to be secured, where the bill of lading could act as a lien on cargo if a situation of default in payment by the Charterer arises. It has been proven most recently in rising cases of cargo theft in US ports, trucking depots, and logistics warehouses that theft is not immune to secured software systems used by logistics and freight forwarding companies, where impersonation of cargo owners requesting goods under immediate payment is a problem. This is where digital systems require intense security guards and server protections that do not exist in the cloud system. This is where the introduction of blockchain use and its security provisions are to stand the test.

Cyberspace attacks, fraud in the online overuse of electronic trade documentation, including financial agreements supported under electronic bills of lading.

Blockchain systems are the software technologies introduced and used in the trade and shipping industry. It is a system that allows parties that have secured access and authority to enter into analyzing the data of shipments being tracked and reported from the point of origin to delivery. Today, blockchain acts as a platform that assists in the transparency and deliverability of crucial information. The conversion of original bills of lading to electronic form exposes carrier to risks in the availability of approved technologies and platforms, since the bill of lading all put data at risk acts as a tangible proof of transfer of goods from one party to another. Payment structures and the number of parties involved in the lending process for financing a cargo shipment, specifically banks as lenders, as silent partners, ensure that funds guarantee the release of the bill of lading to the correct party. During 9/11, internet- based reporting systems were introduced by all border security agencies in entering ports around the world as a security measure to ensure that controls were in place, forcing the workforce in this industry to work with internet

---

[5] The Electronic Trade Document Act 2023, Chapter 38, (UK).

systems versus physical documents. In the name of terrorism or weapons of mass destruction, web-based platforms have now become the method of how public safety would be safeguarded through the internet system of data controls and transparency. The transition was targeting those who operated the system of trade to bring further controls and compliance in order to bring security beyond the capacity of paper documentation. The new global reporting system by vessel carriers has now confirmed a standard of acceptable behaviour of reporting under the terms and conditions of appointed federal agency representatives. This squeezed out smaller exporters and importers, making room for major bankruptcies and mergers, to only make room for those that can survive the demands from higher authorities. The demand to compete, comply, and stabilize revenues while maintaining new software programs under EDI and internet web-based reporting systems for the submission of vessel cargo manifests 48 hours prior to loading squeezed out labor and choice of career services. Today, the legislation enacted specifically in the UK in its adoption of the Electronic Trade Document Act of 2023 forms a model for pushing other nations to follow the same digital priorities. The financial banking system is gaining revenues from investments in digital technologies from the government to big tech, including the spin-off from these assets.

The compatibility requirements facing global carriers and operators, including the charterers with current software systems, go beyond simple upgrades, rather massive encryption coding securing data to be translated and understood by those having security access. The investment in technology software by industry, technology companies, and governments to support new electronic trade documentation needs to take into consideration who is controlling the decisions to employ AI-based machinery. In the push for a digital world of innovation and advancement, who bears the costs, potential revenues in global growth?

The type of AI-powered data running through 6G and 7G, as high as 8G, will have higher transmittable frequencies in the ability to think and answer what is expected. The key question addressed in this section is on the compatibility and current systems used today to adopt a system of electronic transfer. Today, a blockchain-led API and DCSA system of platforms provides data transmission from one person to another, transmitted directly to a platform provider where data is owned and installed exclusively by the principal of the trade transaction. In the case of an Ocean Bill of Lading as a transport and trade document, it would be the vessel carrier, in a contractual service agreement with the shipper of the space, being the cargo owner known as the charterer, that would hold vendor and supplier contracts.

The obligation of the technology company is to ensure all transactions on platforms are secured under their system, which cannot be manipulated or altered by a hacker or outside party. What companies do allow, which brings confidence to the industry using electronic form, is the End-to-End Encryption of Digital Signatures and how to secure non-detachable digital signatures registered in blockchain ledgers to avoid removal. The end-to-end encryption is based on AES Keys and asymmetric (RSA) keys that do not pass through the servers of the platform providers, which allows a secure payment method for trade transactions. The problem is that today's platforms and ledgers used to support such transactions are not all qualifying as reliable and need to be vetted prior to acceptance as a qualifying legal form in each jurisdiction governed by each country that agrees to adopt such a system under their own legal reforms and laws outside of the UK Act of 2023.

What industry regulators are suggesting specifically in the UK, where the Electronic Trade Documentation Act of 2023 has been enacted and enforced, is to have a registry established to assist industry players and stakeholders in choosing a vetted and accredited software company that can fulfill the security requirements of a digitally protected system of transactions. There are limitations to the extent how much control is extended to those in a position to set regulations and rules in the management and control of decisions, including complaints submitted by vessel owners and cargo owners in claims arising from misuse of technology or fraud. How would such cases be handled in terms of reporting damages or losses because of misuse or technical problems with the technology recommended under the guidance of the registry experts? These are valid questions and real-time use case studies that need to be evaluated, vetted, and tested to assure consumers, end users, shippers, and retailers, all acting as third-party interests, are considered and protected.

For example, Maersk and IBM cancelled their initial blockchain-based TradeLens platform, a platform that sought to achieve a complete overhaul of global supply chain digitization. What remains different today, under the UK Act of 2023, is whether it would legally support new DLT-based trade finance products, such as an ocean bill of lading, delivery receipt, or mates' receipt, etc.

In the absence of law for the electronic trade documentation supporting software platforms, the parties would need to agree and incorporate such terms and conditions in their agreements as an equivalent to the UK Act of 2023. This would create rights between the parties while still protecting the transactions under contractual agreements, even under an electronic transmission. The courts still hold the position to decide if the electronic transmission holds the same legal consequences as a paper copy, noting many platforms are still advocating for legal reforms to reflect their products and services offered to the maritime trade industry.

4.1 Stakeholders Promoting Electronic Form Of Ocean Bill Of Lading

The main stakeholder groups that would be impacted in terms of trade and transportation documentation would be the carriers, their operators, freight forwarders, insurance carriers, P and I clubs, and financial lenders of cargo. The push for digital options, specifically the original bill of lading, surrounds financial monetary gains that today would be held back due to the speed of transmitting funds against cargo deliveries supported by a document of ownership. Clearly, the legal reforms required to transition at the jurisdictional level of legal approvals and processes to support the changing of laws are a process of approval at the highest level of authority, and lawmakers need to recognize that monetary gain, technology innovation, and progression are not the only factors to consider.

The economic and legal priorities set in motion to accelerate a global trade documentation system that is electronic and instant in speed have their benefits while having their disadvantages. The financial resources and manpower required to successfully adopt a national or international digital system of trade documentation at a time of high inflation, rising cost of food, housing, energy, and transportation, freight rates, duties, and tariffs, are the largest obstacle. Developing nations should not be subsidized by developed nations in such a project, when their own GDP and loss of industry production, due to carbon taxes on industry, have placed immense undue hardship on the consumer, citizen, and user of the services.

The maritime industry, specifically its regulators and industry associations, including technology companies, has not established a cost projection per carrier in its documentation systems to be replaced under vetting procedures and dedicated time frames to meet such goals. The top container carriers come from maritime subsidized nations, where state budgets set allocations specifically for building a strong and resilient maritime industry, not only in trade but in ship-building and technology advancement.

It is the North American consumer and cargo owner, the shipper, who faces increases in freight rates for imports, specifically from foreign-flagged ships that make up 80% of commercial cargo ships. To what degree will legislators set bills that protect the consumer or their importing businesses from exposure to such price increases, and how will the Shipping Act of the United States and Canada be modified under existing laws to assure a balance of trade?

5.1 Carriage Of Goods Act, Modifications, And Importance Of The Act

The *Carriage of Goods Act by Sea of* 1992 defines under sections 5 and 6 the obligations of the delivery of the carrier with the shipper and the liability of any damages or losses associated with the act of transport.[6]

These sections would need to be omitted to have the electronic trade document have the same legal acceptance as the ocean bill of lading, but this poses a problem for its legal efficacy in the objective of real proof of delivery or misdelivery to another party. These two sections, if removed, would not hold the carrier liable if any damages or losses occurred while under the control of the carrier or goods in their possession. What is important in the relationships carried out between parties in the exchange of cargo are the terms set out under the Charter Party agreement that are not specified on a bill of lading because the bill of lading acts as a transferable receipt to support the physical transfer of cargo from carrier to shipper or it's representative on the other side of the world. This aspect of how maritime law has been written cannot be repealed, nor has it been redefined in its intent and purpose to ensure a paper form of delivery is executed. The Charter Party will address and include aspects of law that govern the contract of service, specifically if a dispute arises and arbitration or legal proceedings need to take place with a jurisdiction nominated by both parties, favorable in time, cost, and travel.

The larger question is whether, under the Carriage of Goods Act, these two sections can be omitted, removing any liability a carrier would have normally under this act to alter its purpose and legal definition in reference to the obligation of performance. To date, no real cases have come forward except cases where banks' consent to release of cargo is required due to the financing of the cargo, as the banks' role is one of lender and owner of the cargo. Financial Institutions, Insurance Carriers, including P and I Clubs, Hull and Machinery, represent the owners' interests in the perils of the seas and the type of risks or exposure a carrier would have in its transit of goods, acting merely as a transferee of goods from carriage to land.

One needs to be prepared to mitigate or foresee these incidents, events, or losses through previous experiences or case studies, especially over time, when new laws and practices are executed, enacted, and tested under real-time applications. The efforts made by the UK in supporting its Act extend to the implementation of the ICC UK's Centre for Digital Trade and Innovation, currently working towards a

---

[6] Electronic Trade Documentation Act 2023, Chapter 38, (UK).

model that supports a reliable system. Its influence or extension of mandating standards to other nations through its efforts to build a centralized registry for all to use and model, regardless of jurisdiction, points to no competition. This is one problem the maritime leading nations have created specifically in their colonization of green technology and digitalization on a global scale. The UK and EU countries have sustained and invested over the last 40 years in a global fleet of maritime carriers servicing trade around the world, relying on foreign ports and terminals for carrying out trade. Reference is made by the EU to the enormous amount of potential revenues that the new technology would create in the global maritime system, but it does not provide a concrete understanding of how and where the trillions would be sourced.

The Commonwealth report on the Quantitative Analysis of the Movement to Paperless Trade, predicts it could increase trade in the Commonwealth by USD $1 .2 trillion by 2026.[7]

6.1 Regulatory Direction, Accommodation, And Jurisdictional Approvals

The largest institutions impacted by the UK Electronic Trade Documentation Act of 2023 in the UK are the Trade Banks and Insurance Carriers. They are directly linked to trade financing transactions from seller to buyer under letters of credit and secured ship financing agreements.

Today, we have letters of credit providing financial security in risky markets as an assurance that payment against documents will be upheld under well-defined terms and conditions accepted by foreign and domestic banks. Electronic Trade documentation may not be recognized in these foreign jurisdictions, specifically under their banking rules and legislation, especially in developing nations. The financial stability of the trading bank and its governments needs to be stable and trusted, specifically if rules are to reflect new regulatory and technical changes adopted under a new set of regulatory standards and procedures.

It is imperative that assigning legal responsibility between vendor and carrier relationships is clear, specifically in cases where technical issues, problems with interoperability, adoption, and transfer of data develop. Documentation processes and procedures would require the leadership of experienced managers who have worked through previous technical regulatory changes introduced by industry due to global events or technology advancements, as we see today. Interoperability has its boundaries in parties seeking to protect their commercial information while assuring that data transfer from carrier to shipper and shipper to carrier can perform well in its exchange.

The human element of communications on both sides of the relationship and progression is key as documentation systems, IT specialists, vendor providers, and the engineering team work together to meet end goals. New P and I coverages are defined for each unique and independent club, requiring new risks to be brokered. Risk previously nonexistent under paper form has now arisen in a new world of internet risks, specifically misrepresentation of information, impersonation of a buyer, fraud, and criminal rings declaring goods and payment under false claims. How are these incidents traced in terms of documentation and any evidence that leads to criminal evidence, individuals involved, originating transactions, authority

---

[7] Hill Dickinson, UK's Electronic Trade Documentation Act, October 13, 2023,
https://www.hilldickinson.com/insights/articles/uks-electronic-trade-documents-act-now-force

in releasing funds, and a bill of lading against delivery?

Lastly, jurisdiction approvals and recognition of electronic form need to be interchangeable with paper form instantaneously without delay, which is a feature most systems will need to have to avoid penalties or delays.

7.1 New Standards And Practices

The monetary benefits of an electronic system are very clear, but the trade-off in other areas of growth, such as human creativity, investment in software, and benefits to the public, taxpayers, and investors in returns, have not been identified. For example, it has been made clear that 6.5 billion direct cost savings and 40 billion in increased trade revenues are what can be gained through the implementation of an electronic document system.[8]

Technology advancements in this area of electronic trade documentation have set new standards and practices that are required to match those of the original bill of lading. They are defined below as the following prerequisites.

1. **Legality and Recognition.**

   E-BLs are fully recognized as equivalent to paper Bills of Lading with the same functions.

2. **Receipt of Goods.**

   Endure the contract of carriage and its document title. Contact information is fully captured as an original Bill of Lading, such as shipper, consignee, description, quantity, units, shipping terms, load port, discharge port, in transit options, carrier terms and conditions surrounding COGSA terms.

3. **Reliability and Control, Integrity.**

   Exclusive control of documents can be managed through their validity.

   What do we mean by this word? The actual measures to maintain the integrity of electronic records. Prevent unauthorized access or alteration.

4. **Transferability.**

   Must be transferable, allowing the title to be transferred to another party.

5. **Compliance with regulations.**

   Meets all legal standards.

The current framework created by DCSA that can deliver on the E-bill of lading essentially has three

---

[8] DCSA Completes Standards-based Implementation, EBL transactions marking a major Industry milestone. Mar 15, 2025, dcsa.org/newsroom/ebl-interoperability-milestone.

critical components, which are listed below.[9]

1. **Platform Integrity.**

   Assuring security and compatibility with Solution Providers.

2. **Legal Framework.**

   Multi-Lateral Agreement, which includes the relationships between EBL solutions, providers, and users in a standard format.

3. **Log Tracking.**

   E-Bl trust building for global trade.

The key rule that best establishes the proposed E-BL system is best defined as a set of standards and benefits that benefit the enterprise, its human resources, training programs, and returns to corporate and domestic welfare. This brings us to the benefits that have been calculated by DCSA, BIMCO, in monetary terms rather than social, consumer, or end user benefits equally shared in reducing freight rates, inflationary rises, and increased fuel levies not warranted. The International parameters of law of binding agreements between member states in a global reboot of all digital systems, reflective of documentation, compromises the human element of communication, employment, and accountability. The legal aspect of removing liability from carriers in their obligation to meet delivery standards and practices is also, at some point, reversed to ensure technology providers earn their mark in the sector. What has not been pointed out by the three groups specifically the Digital Container Shipping Association, BIMCO, and the Motor Freight Traffic Association is who gains the benefits of these monetary returns or cost savings. Historically, during upswings of market performance, the vessel owners and their agents/carriers have not cut freight rates or held back surcharges when innovation or technology were applied to vessel operations.

In fact, following 9/11 price increases, were put in place, due to online reporting requirements by federal and state authorities of cargo shipments, passed onto the cargo owner and later filtered down to the end consumer. Today, carbon tax regimes are leading to higher transport costs, as most recently noted by carriers' recent increase due to carbon taxes. Legitimately, the facts above relate solely to economics, which is part of the equation, but the other factors in terms of legal and commercial benefits remain.

The key aspects of rules governing such a new system are comparable to the rules governing original bills of lading under paper copy, but the other factors such as "consumer rights" and anti-trust laws question legitimacy of increases. which are security controls that make it better, data accuracy and integrity, fraud prevention, visibility, and training, while all protecting the rights of the owner. Methods of identification and controlling records are so important, along with major communication about what data is required as information to avoid legal disputes arising out of loss, delays, damages, and misdeliveries.

The purpose of electronic is to keep records of all information as the paper copy does today, including changes to holder, owner, and transferee of the bill of lading that direct the trade activity

---

[9] DCSA Completes Standards-based Implementation, EBL transactions marking a major Industry milestone. Mar 15, 2025, dcsa.org/newsroom/ebl-interoperability-milestone.

of the actual consignment in multiple jurisdictions and transit points. Visibility to shippers has been denied in terms of making it known to shipper that a vessel has diverse routings, transshipment points, and delays because of preferred profitable routes. Multiple trade routes are not identified in a straight through bill of lading vessel positioning, port changes are not fully transparent in electronic bill of lading specifically port calls terminals and trade routes including historical data on vessel activities.

Insurance carriers, banking partners, and regulators play a large part in the financial equation of commercial financing of commodities and goods from origin to end-point delivery, as we see in letters of credit, approved financing through third-party loans.

8.1 Creating A Reliable Trade Electronic Document System

The dilemma facing industry and its regulators is the ability to provide legal weight equally to an electronic paper document as one does to the paper original copy. Regardless of technology and its ability to increase value monetarily in its trade volumes and applications to benefit its investors, the legal judicial system and legislation in place today cannot be modified to provide the same legal weight of the paper copy to the electronic copy.

The clear definition of a reliable system that constitutes an electronic trade document today needs to meet the following criteria:

1. Contains the same information as its paper equivalent

2. It is distinguishable from other copies.

3. Is protected against unauthorized alteration

4. Is access-restricted in a way that ensures only one person can exercise control over it at any one time

5. Is sufficiently accessible that a person who can exercise control over it can demonstrate this; and

6. Is fully divested on transfer - i.e., is only transferable in a way that grants the transferee exclusive control, which cannot be shared with the transferor.[10]

As the regulators continue encouraging collaboration and commitments from all parties in changing current trade documentation systems to conform and adapt to new standards, the reality of how standards are measured over time in their benefits is another challenge. We need to identify the key mechanisms and ways to measure outcomes over time of these standards based on what works for each jurisdiction or nation, depending on their trade systems, resources, regulations, governance structures, and industry tools. Of the actual financing and possession of goods that are transferable electronically. What is being missed in this process of transferring assets, specifically physical commodities, from buyer to seller in the use of a maritime trade document, is the requirement of a reliable system. If the industry requires security measures to be adopted under a new system of possession that is electronic, the financing channels of

---

[10] Clifford Chance, UK Electronic Trade Documents Act 2023: A further step towards paperless trade. July 22, 2025, www.cliffordchance.com.

deposits and payments need to work the same way. What we see today is a large number of SME's who are not getting in the gate due to market share being saturated by companies controlling the share of market revenues and able to meet green requirements as part of the technology objective.

9.1 State, Federal, And International Adoption Of Electronic Trade Documentation

Other nations outside the UK have adopted their own model of adoption of electronic trade documentation, specifically in the transfer of possession of goods under a commercial contract agreement outside of the charter party agreement. For example, Singapore has adopted the MLETR model of electronic trade documentation as a regional leader in trade, noting its banking system is linking favorable loans to those trading companies using software to measure delivery of bunkering fuels approved under clean energy requirements. Nations such as China, Japan, and South Korea have taken a different approach, following domestic legislation setting out how electronic documents may be owned and transferred to shippers or clients, outlining specifically what rights and entitlements such documents entail.

The objective of the UN under its development of the modern law trade records (MLETR) is to bring a gradual legal globalized system of one set of standards that all jurisdictions would adopt in modeling the UK Act, noting that the UK Act only pertains to English law trade documents. The UN MLETR used the Rotterdam Rules of 2008 principles in how it internationally standardized liability for loss and damages a party faced under the carriage of goods at sea. Having success in adopting its principles, the rules of possession and title of goods hold different legal significance in establishing the cause of damage and loss, and who is liable, versus ownership of cargo and its financial transactions to support the trade.

Moving forward with the established UK Act of 2023 and its laws does set a precedent for the UK jurisdiction, but not that of other nations, specifically non-common law nations that have not adopted UK law under their contractual agreement of maritime charter parties. What has not been set is the other nations that have not agreed to such a system of electronic trade documentation.

Foreign banks and insurance carriers are most affected as institutions in the group of major stakeholders that decide if one form is accepted over the other, and on the receiving and distributing side of the original bill of lading documents. The electronic system of trade documentation has been tested in the Singapore jurisdiction for domestic trade activities. Interoperability of the paper form and the electronic form must meet the same criteria, including purpose, ownership, title of cargo, and legal efficacy. How you can manage and vet the system adopted by the carrier in your transportation agreement is by requesting which systems have been tested and approved by regulators in each trading jurisdiction.

Keeping close relations with vendors and suppliers within your own jurisdiction is key, specifically in their understanding of the risks and liabilities you face as a buyer or seller of goods if the software system is disrupted, or they fail to perform due to software outages or repairs in the marketplace. Advocating for or having someone within your organization to present your needs as an international exporter, shipper of a product requiring maritime transportation to global markets, who understands well the regulatory and legislative rules set out under an electronic trade system, is of great value.

It is important to grasp the basis of the model put forward by the UK, specifically the United Nations, ICS, and BIMCO, which is called the UNICITRAL Model Law on Electronic Transferable Records (MLETR). The jurisdictional approvals specific to a state in the USA that do not recognize UN-based standards, due to the model law not being actual laws enacted by the state itself, are warranted and very much justified in refuting electronic bills of lading.

10.1 International And National Legal Reforms

Today, 54 common-law countries are exposed to the influence and adoption under the UK Act of 2023 as a model law, not actual laws, to have their own judiciary and parliamentary system implement substantial reforms. The advancements require reforms to acknowledge the legitimacy of the electronic document, which is the struggle facing most jurisdictions. The loophole that is considered most risky to the rule of law is the interchangeability of rules from international private law to the Electronic Trade Act of the UK, because it allows a country to use its influence in a way that benefits its own country judicially. It oversteps the principles supporting private contractual law in the international arena, which is not controlled by the UK as a nation.

Regardless of the transferability or interoperability of paper to electronic, on the cross-border aspects of movement of goods under the trade documents, cross-border needs to deal with the actual domestic legislation of that jurisdiction in its contractual agreements. What is most evident and used to assure commercial risk is covered are express laws and jurisdictional clauses as part of the charter party agreement between the carrier and shipper.

The international significance of the UK Act of 2023 is in its model of transferability from a paper copy to an electronic copy, specifically in its application to transport documents such as the bill of lading. What is being proposed by the UK parliament and industry is to have a registry established with suggested IT software companies that are recognized as reliable by the operating carriers and trade regulations, including state regulators. This system would be controlled, managed, and funded by the UK government through a process of assessment and audit, and implementation of a registry including reliable software systems to assist users in choosing a credible system.

The Act impacts a large percentage of international shipping and trade contracts as the majority are governed by English Law, specifically for common law countries, which are major trading and maritime nations.

To keep in mind is that the jurisdictions outside the UK do not carry this same law, nor the obligation to accept this law in a foreign court of judgment. To date, we do not have any examples specifically of legal disputes arising from the interoperability of paper to electronic documentation in G7 countries, as it is at its very early stages of implementation or use.

Singapore, for example, has used electronic trade documentation at the regional level of maritime trade, not reporting at this time any arbitration awards or legal cases put forward through its court systems. The push for G7 countries to adopt a law that reflects that of the UK Act of 2023 is in the best interests of monetarily, the stakeholders, financial systems and insurance carriers benefit from reducing costs and saving time on acceptance by regular wire transfer systems.

For example, in the Commonwealth report on the Quantitative Analysis of the movement to Paperless Trade, it is predicted that digitalization could increase trade in the Commonwealth by $1.2 trillion by 2026.[11]

How this is to trans fold has not been researched or concluded with facts through this workbook, but may be through other resources.

New instruments and international conventions have been pushed and continue to be pushed by the United Nations, working with the commonwealth nations, specifically the UK, where new instruments in the form of international conventions will provide legal recognition of negotiable multimodal transport documents like negotiable bills of lading.[12]

These changes would make a trade document from buyer and seller under a commercial contract, hold the same function and purpose legally, as a transport document, specifically a negotiable Bill of Lading. Another key characteristic is that goods sold while transiting over water could be sold using these very documents, with the buyer on the other side of the world holding the risk of damages or losses while in transit.

Lawmakers and regulators of the UK and other G7 Commonwealth countries need to be careful in assuring any new conventions do not compromise any existing conventions regulating the carriage of goods by sea, such as the Hague-Visby Rules, COGSA, and the Hamburg Rules. This is a voluntary system in which choice is paramount, with some carriers having adopted a standard bill of lading based on recommendations made by BIMCO, supporting global vessel owners around the world as members. When carriers commit to exclusive use of electronic bills by 2030, it raises concerns about costs, affordability, controls, surveillance targeting consumers, end users, retailers, shippers, exporters, and producers, including the financial and insurance institutions.

When 9/11 occurred, carriers were forced to report via electronic transmission of data to Homeland Security and to the Canadian Border Services Agency, where the rest of the world followed in investing millions into a new global system, each being recognized as a requirement of entry. This had a negative effect on trade accuracy, data verifications, delays, and questionable penalties used to only undermine the legitimate system of trade and shipping, where goods were being moved according to description, quantity, and quality as per the bill of lading.

This legal requirement pushed out smaller players in the market who did not have the capacity, capital, human resources, training tools, or budgets to conform to new compliance regulations, which only created less choice to the consumer in the selection of carriers in the marketplace. This also pushed freight prices upwards, resulting in higher freight rates for the cargo owners, their shippers, as a result of the increased regulations led by the maritime industry and its G7 governments.

---

[11] Hill Dickinson, UK's Electronic Trade Documentation Act now in force, October.
[12] 13, 2023, https://www.hilldickinson.com/insights/articles/uks-electronic-trade-documents-act-now-force.

11.1 Applicable Case Law And New York Arbitration Awards

Neutral Citation No: [2022] EWHC 957 (comm.) Case No: CL-2021-000020

Date: 28/04/2022

In the High Court of Justice, Business and Property Courts Of England and Wales, Commercial Court (QBD)

Claimant: UNICREDIT BANK A.G.

Defendant: Euronav N.V

Parties to the Agreement

Switz Bank Charterer - Euronav

Captain Philippine, De Manager Master of the vessel voyage

Finance Agreements

2019 - Bank agrees to Gulf Stream exporter/shipper, December 18, 2019, facility agreement

Back and Gulf, deed and pledge assignment, Direct payment sub-buyer to the bank.

Key Issue

Did the Bill of Lading contain or provide evidence, a contract of carriage of goods, on or after April 6, 2020? Prior to the alleged agreement (Novation Agreement of April 6, 2025 did this bill of lading act as a commercial contract to determine the liability of the parties of cargo released against bank financing of a portion of Gulf Oil?

Key Complaint

Carrier attains contractual status upon endorsement based on a new contract. The Bank Uni Credit did not receive an endorsed original bill of lading upon request, as the carrier and BP hold a commercial relationship, having originals sent to the London, UK BP commercial office. Endorsed bills were not received by to Gulf at any point until August 2020.

Bank claims commercial contract had no legal bearing on the bill of lading, the carriage of goods act, or agreement, specifically to the Novation agreement in place versus the charter party agreement.

The bill acted merely as a transfer of rights to obligations under the charter party from BP to Gulf. BP and the owner, reloading the dissolved liability of the bill of lading.

Judges' Review

Key points addressed: Bill acts as a mere receipt of transferred goods in the absence of an express clause in the bill of lading, intention of parties to separate contract of commercial agreement of sale from to bill of lading as a carriage of goods contract.

Issue of Contention

Whether claimant losses are warranted due to the decision to have oil shipped from the vessel under STS transfer from the carrier, BP, Gulf, and Uni Credit, due to the terminal having all tanks full at the nominated port of discharge in Asia.

If the good was transferred to the tank at the nominated terminal, would the claimant have incurred loss regardless of circumstances such as Covid impacts on congestion at port, labor delays, shortage of staff, and delay of OBL from the BP corporate office in London?

The circumstances, events, and facts that surround this claim were all considered by the Judge, noting his summary below.

The owner was aware and BP that it would not make economic sense under industry practice to have parcels of 5,000 to 6,000 mt for such small transfers.

This is not a normal standard of industry practice for the tanker business, as the vessel type Suez Max is are large tanker with larger volumes.

Issue

Whether it was part of the general agreement or would have been agreed or permitted by the Bank, as part of a general agreement.

Consider the view of the bank representative in putting COVID as a cause to not allow ports to be accessed, and the logistics of cargo transfer. All others are in the same predicament with shipments.

The issue facing the courts is whether the failure by the Owners to require production of the Bill of Lading caused the loss or whether the Bank would have suffered the same loss.

Conclusion Summary

The Bank had no specific concern that the Gulf would fall into default in payment for the bank financing of the cargo.

Gulf had taken out trade credit insurance covering 90% of the receivables under the contracts with the Sub buyers and had confirmed that they were acceptable, and by 4 May 2020, had received the invoices.

Based on Economic circumstances, assessment of the credibility of Ms. Bodnya, and in the circumstances discussed, including the impact of COVID, the decision by the judge was based on the following evidence.

1) The claimant did permit and, in any event, would have permitted discharge without production of the Bill of Lading.

2) The Claimant would have permitted discharge at Sohar by STS.

3) If the Claimant had been aware, or told that discharge was to be made by STS at Sohar, the Claimant would not have halted discharge and would have carried out investigations into Gulf and /or Sub-buyers.

4) The loss would have occurred in any event.

5) Lastly, any breach by the owners in discharging the financed cargo without production of the Bill of Lading did not cause the loss, or in the alternative, that the Bank would have occurred in any event.

Judge Decision

Breach by the owners in discharging the Financed Cargo without production of the Bill of Lading did not cause the loss, or, in the alternative, that the Bank would have suffered the same loss in any event.

Arbitration Awards, USA District Court, S.D. New York - two cases below, as references.

553 F. Supp. 2d 328 United States District Court, S.D. New York.

PADRE SHIPPING INC., PLAINTIFF, V YONG, HE SHIPPING, a/k/a Yong He Shipping (HK) Limited; Prosper Shipping Limited; Shanghai Cosfar Shipping International Co. Ltd.; Aegean Carriers SA.

Synopsis.

Background: Liberian vessel owner brought action against Chinese port agent, alleging claim for breach of authorization letter based on its issuance of unauthorized bills of lading, and seeking maritime attachment and garnishment against port agent to obtain security for contemplated arbitration in London and litigation in China. The port agent moved to vacate the process of maritime attachment and to release funds that had been attached, and to dismiss the complaint.

Holdings: The District Court held that:

1. The vessel owner showed that it had a valid prima facie admiralty claim against the port agent, and

2. The port agent had an attachable property interest in restrained funds.

204 F. Supp. 2d 675 United States District Court, S.D. NewYork.

CENTRAL NATIONAL - GOTTESMAN INC. Plaintiff V M.V. GERTRUDE OLDENDORFF, her engines, boilers, etc., and EO Oldendorff, Defendants. No. Oo Civ. 6425 (RLC).

No. Oo Civ. 6425 (RLC)1

May 22, 2002.

Synopsis

The shipper brought action against the vessel to recover for damage to the shipment. On the vessel's motion to dismiss, the district court, Robert L. Carter, J., held that the mandatory forum selection clause in the bill of lading was not enforceable.

Background

September 24th, 1999, defendant Oldendorff issued a bill of lading, numbered LCLB-1, for the carriage and transportation of 1,735 rolls of fluting paper, allegedly tendered in good order and condition, aboard the vessel M.V. Gertrude Oldendorff from the port of Laem Chabang. Thailand to the port of Long Beach, California.

The MV GERTRUDE OLDENDORFF

On October 22, 1999, the M.V. Gertrude Oldendorff arrived at the port of Long Beach, California, and defendant Oldendorff discharged plaintiffs' shipment of fluting paper. Upon inspection, it was discovered that the shipment had sustained serious physical and water damage. The damaged rolls were subsequently segregated and sold for salvage.

Plaintiff Gottesman, as owner, shipper, consignee, and purchaser of the aforesaid shipment of 1,735 rolls of fluting paper, instituted this action on its behalf and on behalf of all other interested parties to recover the sum of $600,000 for damage sustained to the shipment. On January 26, 2001, plaintiff Gottesman also commenced an action in the High Court of Justice, Queen's Bench Division, London, UK, in which the registered owner of the vessel, New Resolution Shipping Corp., is named as a defendant.

Summary DECISION For CENTRAL NATIONAL- GOTTESMAN INC. Plaintiff v. M.V. Gertrude Oldendorff Synopsis.

Shipper brought action against the vessel to recover for damage to the shipment. On the Vessel's motion to dismiss, the District Court held that the mandatory forum selection clause in the bill of lading was not enforceable.

Summary of reasons behind the decision. Applicable Legislation.

1) **Presumption and Burden of Proof.**

   The plaintiff bears the burden of showing that the venue is proper once it has been challenged.

2) **Agreement as to place of bringing suit; forum selection clauses.**

   Forum selection clauses in admiralty law are presumptively valid.

The presumption of Validity attached to a mandatory forum selection clause may be overcome by clearly showing that the clause is unreasonable.

Mandatory forum selection clauses can be unreasonable if: Part of the agreement includes fraud or overreach.

The complaining party would be denied its day in court due to the inconvenience of the selected forum.

Chosen law is completely unfair to deprive the plaintiff of a remedy; the Clause is in strong contravention of public remedy, or the clause is in contravention of a strong public policy of the forum state.

Damages pertain to 1735 rolls of fluting paper. The carrier acting as defendant removes to dismiss the complaint for improper venue. This motion and the reasons set below.

Forum selection clause requiring any disputes under Bill of Lading to be decided in London, according to English Law, mandatory, in nature, precluded suit in the USA to recover for damage to shipment, provided not unjust and unreasonable

3) **Legal remedies and proceedings.**

For a forum selection clause to be deemed mandatory, jurisdiction and venue must be specified with mandatory or exclusive language.

Situation where only jurisdiction is specified, mandatory language needs to be provided that indicates the intent of the parties to make jurisdiction exclusive to make it enforceable.

4) **Agreements on the place of bringing suit, forum of selection clauses.**

Key information that plays a factor is within the bill of lading clause, where UK courts perceive the exculpatory clause in the bill of lading as insulating parties other than the shipowner from liability. The law in this case would act as a waiver of the shipper's rights to pursue statutory remedies under the Carriage of Goods Act of Sea (COGSA) was not enforceable due to English Law would give preference to the exclapatory clause in the bill of lading that supports owners in removing all liabilities. The US court in this case would have no opportunity to review the English Courts' decision to ensure that it comported with COGSA, specifically sections 2, 3 (8) 46 APP U.S.C.A section 1302 and 1303 (8). Sourcing such maritime Law in their own country, providing a constructive, informed picture of how a foreign court may approach this decision.

Background of why this reason was brought forward.

Bill of lading issued by carrier/defendant Oldendorff for carriage and transportation 1,735 rolls of fluting paper in good order and condition on MV GERTRUDE OLDENDORFF from the port of Laem Chabang, Thailand to the port of Long Beach, California.

Voyage controlled, owned, operated, and chartered by defendant Oldendorff. Noted damage of roles, time of discharge, and of inspection, at this point, Segregated roles sold for the salvage market. The plaintiff is the owner, consignee, and shipper of Rolls of fluting paper pursued action on behalf of other interested parties and themselves. When considering a motion to dismiss improper venues pursuant to Rule 12 (b) (3) F.R. Civ. P, the court needs to accept facts alleged as true, construe all reasonable inferences in favor of the plaintiff. The plaintiff ultimately bears the burden of showing that venue is proper once it has been challenged. Clause 3 of the bill of lading provides that all the adjudicated disputes be put in front of the London court. The carrier identifies where the forum clause is in the bill of lading, specifically how it is mandatory and exclusive to the bill of lading clause. Regardless of assuming exclusivity, the presumption of validity attached to a forum selection clause may be overcome by a clear clause showing it is unreasonable. Did the judge find the clause to be unreasonable in this case after considering the following points?

1. **Fraud or overreaching;**

2. **Deprived in court due to its inconvenience of the select forum clause**

3. **The chosen law is manifestly unfair so as to deprive the plaintiff of a remedy.**

4. **The clause is in strong contravention of a strong public policy of the forum state.13**

---

13 Central National-Gottesman, Inc. v. M.V. "Gertrude Oldendorff". 204 F. Supp. 2d 675, United States District Court. S.D. New York.

What is important to distinguish in this case is whether the situation shows only that jurisdiction was specified with no explicit language to make jurisdiction exclusive. If mandatory venue language is employed, then it will be enforced even in the absence of language making the jurisdiction exclusive.

The clause being considered in this case is one that states "any disputes under the Bill of landing to be decided in London according to English Law, rather than in any other court and nowhere else.

In comparing this clause to others in similar situations of jurisdiction, in other decisions rendered, it is necessary that the forum selection clause in this case is mandatory and therefore, enforceable, if it is not unreasonable and unjust. The plaintiff Gottesman, according to the reasonable and unjust principle, argues that Oldendorf's liability would be lessened as a carrier under the Carriage of Goods at Sea Act (COGSA or the Act). 46 U.S.C. App section 1300 et seq., thereby undermining the Act and violating public policy [14]

Basically, a section of COGSA states, "Any clause, covenant, or agreement in a contract of carriage relieving the carrier or the ship from liability or loss or damage to or in connection with the goods or lessening such liability otherwise than as provided in this chapter, shall be null and void and of no effect. In the Case of KY REEFER involving a foreign arbitration clause, its reasoning extended to a forum selection clause as well. What was concluded in the case of SKY REEFER is that an arbitration clause is generally a subset of foreign forum selection clauses. Although SKY REEFER extended to an arbitration clause, its reasoning extended to foreign select clauses as well as seen in the case of **Siligan Plastics Corp. vs M/V Nedlloyd Holland, No. 96 Civ. 6188, 1988**

WL 193079, at *2 (S.D.N.Y. Apr.22, 1998).[15]

In this case court is convinced that the forum selection clause at issue is essentially operated as a prospective waiver of Gottesman's right to pursue statutory remedies under COGSA. If case decided in London, instead of US district, strong likelihood that English courts would give force to an exculpatory clause in the bill oflading, insulating The definition of the carrier who holds the actual contract of carriage of goods directly with the shipper, does not Line Company or agents who have executed Bill of Lading for and on behalf of the Master is not a principal in the transaction. In this being said, these parties should not be responsible for any liability arising out of this contract of carriage, nor as a carrier or bailee of goods.

It is made clear under the above case analysis and supporting case law made under the district courts within the United States of America, recovery under COGSA is predicated on a plaintiff's ability to prove a breach of contract of carriage against a carrier of the cargo.

Go to 46 U.S.C. App Section 1302.

Courts in this district have construed the term to expand to include all owners and charterers participating in the carriage of goods seen in the example ofJoo Seng Hong Kong Co., Ltd. V. S.S.

---

14 Central National-Gottesman, Inc. v. M.V. "Gertrude Oldendorff". 204 F. Supp. 2d 675, United States District Court. S.D. New York

[15] Central National-Gottesman, Inc. v. M.V. "Gertrude Oldendorff". 204 F. Supp. 2d 675, United States District Court. S.D. New York.

Unibulkfir, 483 F. Supp. 43 (S.D.N.Y. 1979).[16]

The court noted that more than one party is often found liable to a cargo interest pursuant to the COGSA bill of lading, where there can be more than one COGSA carrier in any given shipment, as seen on bills of lading or cargo in transit through bulk feeder vessels under a specific voyage schedule. Some courts in various districts have not held back from imposing liabilities on charterers or owners that are not signatories to a bill of lading or have issued the bill of lading.

Importantly, the COGSA rule has not been limited to one party; rather, all owners and charterers are involved in the carriage of goods at issue within the bill of lading itself. The COGSA statute has been deliberately drawn to not limit the term to a party to the contract of carriage or the bill of lading.

Important point made by the defendant in this case, "M.V Oldendorff", the carrier, despite finding under the case of Joo Seng, that Joo Seng should not control the court's decision under the Fifth Circuit holding in Thyseen Steel Co. V. M/V KAVO YERMAKOS, 50 F. 3rd 1349 (5th Circuit 1995), rejecting Joo Seng's reasoning.[17]

A key point critical in this district is that a clear definition has been assessed on the term "carrier" in associated carrier liability to the COGSA statute and the breadth of law in defining this. This brings a clear understanding of how the plaintiffs would be relinquishing rights to claim liabilities under the bill of lading under A FORUM where COGSA would not be applicable. In this case, the forum clause would jeopardize and violate COGSA. This would be sufficient grounds to allow the court to retain jurisdiction over the case.

The foreign lawyers who have been responsive to the law in their foreign countries, specifically on the COGSA forum of liabilities, provided an informed picture of how courts would approach the term of carrier on an issue of the selection forum clause.

Japanese and Chinese attorneys familiar with court decisions in their own jurisdiction have seen incidents where courts may apply the clause in the bill of lading to defend the defendants' obligations, reducing the threshold set by COGSA.

The central guarantee of section 3(8) is that the terms of the bill of lading may not relieve the carrier of the obligations or diminish its legal duties specified by the Act itself. [18]

This bill is created by the industry specifically for vessel owners' representatives under trade associations such as BIMCO, ICS, or Baltic Maritime Exchange, who develop the clauses and their standards according to what best defends their members, the vessel owners.

The relevant question brought forward in the above analysis and facts being brought forward in this

---

[16] Central National-Gottesman, Inc. v. M.V. "Gertrude Oldendorff". 204 F. Supp. 2d 675, United States District Court. S.D. New York.
[17] Central National-Gottesman, Inc. v. M.V. "Gertrude Oldendorff". 204 F. Supp. 2d 675, United States District Court. S.D. New York.
[18] Central National-Gottesman, Inc. v. M.V. "Gertrude Oldendorff". 204 F. Supp. 2d 675, United States District Court. S.D. New York.

case, specifically in the US 5th circuit, under a supported COGSA forum, is whether a foreign substantive law applied would reduce carriers' obligation to the cargo owner below what COGSA guarantees.[19]

What has been pointed out in the decision held by the circuit court is regardless of the preference for foreign laws over domestic law, no party subject to COGSA coverage should enjoy protection short of what the Act guarantees. This cannot be compromised to uphold the full use and extent of the law in its practical sense.[20]

This court considered, before making its decision, the decision rendered under the foreign court for the sole purpose of assuring the foreign court decision would conform with the interests of the laws in the United States for enforcement, while not violating public policy.

If it did not have the chance to review the foreign decision, it would have had a much harder time enforcing the forum selection clause, while running the possibility of waiving the COGSA protection while violating the public policy of the United States. Retaining jurisdiction is not the case in this court, as, unlike SKY REEFER, this case involves a foreign jurisdiction clause, not a dispute over the arbitration enforcement of a foreign arbitration clause.[21]

A further difference was articulated by this district, where, in the past, cases where COGSA cases were dismissed due to improper venue.[22]

In cases of this sort, previous cases arose where the plaintiff argued that a foreign forum would apply a more restrictive definition of forum, not allowing the plaintiff to sue only the owner and the time charterer for damages or loss. In some cases, the plaintiff was not put at a disadvantage, as the law of the country, taking Korea as an example, would still allow a defendant to be sued as a carrier, and the plaintiff could also sue the owner in the district.

In the case of a defendant claiming a time statute limitation within a year has passed, the court has made use of substantive law that would not lead to obliterating a carrier's liability or obligation in violation of COGSA law. A case can also be dismissed due to the jurisdictional application of the COGSA Act, as it is limited to vessels calling and operating in US ports. Further consideration taken in the plaintiff jurisdictional choice is an action in rem, where a vessel is not yet arrested, and the case can be taken to the foreign court without depriving the plaintiff of damages in the foreign jurisdiction in exercising COGSA benefits.

Based on all the above circumstances, taken into consideration, the court is convinced that the plaintiff has fulfilled its burden of showing that the forum selection clause in the bill of lading is unreasonable and venue is proper in this district.[23]

---

[19] Central National-Gottesman, Inc. v. M.V. "Gertrude Oldendorff". 204 F. Supp. 2d 675, United States District Court. S.D. New York.

[20] Central National-Gottesman, Inc. v. M.V. "Gertrude Oldendorff". 204 F. Supp. 2d 675, United States District Court. S.D. New York.

[21] Central National-Gottesman, Inc. v. M.V. "Gertrude Oldendorff". 204 F. Supp. 2d 675, United States District Court. S.D. New York.

[22] Central National-Gottesman, Inc. v. M.V. "Gertrude Oldendorff". 204 F. Supp. 2d 675, United States District Court. S.D. New York.

[23] Central National-Gottesman, Inc. v. M.V. "Gertrude Oldendorff". 204 F. Supp. 2d 675, United States District Court. S.D. New York

Closing Summary

The Ocean Bill of Lading, since its inception, has functioned as a document of exchange and transfer of cargo between the carrier and the cargo owner, which is the shipper. The recent push for digital documentation on a global scale by the EU, UK, including Singapore, has been possible due to recent technological advancements in the marketplace. Previously, blockchain and EDI systems of transfer of data transfer replaced the manual entry of paper copies. The interoperability of a document system on a regional, national, and international scale is where bottlenecks and challenges exist. Ocean bills of lading are defined as receipts in the release of cargo to the defined owner or buyer of the cargo, including its representative, who is held by the issuer, being the carrier or freight forwarder. Identifying the parties in the global supply chain of maritime trade is critical in the transfer of title and liability each party bears in the service contract agreement, including terms outlined in the Charter Party agreement. Most importantly, the carrier identified in the Ocean bill of lading can be more than one party, whether owner, carrier, or agent involved in the loading, discharge of cargo, having some part in this activity operationally, or under agreements. The US courts have made decisions involving a clear definition of what constitutes a carrier in terms of any liabilities they bear under the bill of lading clauses, regardless of whether a party to this agreement is named under the bill of lading transport document.

Legislation under the Electronic Trade Documentation UK Act of 2023 concerns itself primarily with the technology functions and purpose it serves in the rapid transfer of large blocks of data, legalizing this process under the same legal integrity as the "Ocean Bill of Lading" and its qualities. The legal force and purpose of both statutes, that is, the Carriage of Goods Act by Sea of 1992 and the UK Act of 2023, encompass trade documentation in the commercialization, financing, and payment of goods through maritime trade.

The legal and commercial implications of the transport contract, specifically between carrier and shipper, are in its obligations of performance that the owner of the bill of lading needs to carry out. How the owner or carrier is identified in terms of legal obligation outlined under the Bill of Lading and the Carriage of Goods Act of 1992 has been tested by the US and Foreign court decisions in legal disputes of loss and damages, as mentioned earlier in the book. One can conclude, in this analysis, that the differences in applications of both documents in how they are used in the practical sense, as a transfer of title document, hold a unique quality that other trade documents do not have, specifically under the transport contract.

This is demonstrated under the Carriage of Goods by Sea Act of 1992, supported by international maritime law, referencing specifically articles 5 and 6, holding vessel owners liable for any damages or losses to cargo while under their possession during the voyage, while in transit.

It is required that the UK Act of 2023, as model law, encompasses articles 5 and 6, to ensure the electronic form does not compromise this condition, which is a requirement and quality of the original bill of lading in paper form. Terms and conditions under a separate commercial agreement, including the Charter Party agreement under the transport document, should be added to not remove carrier liability under articles 5 and 6.

The legal efficacy of the original signed bill of lading needs to be maintained under the new form which cannot be compromised, specifically under the electronic form. How is this task accomplished? Regulatory regimes created by industry and regulators have responded to laws such as the UK Act of 2023, as Singapore in assured minimum standards and practices are established. For example, the UK has proposed establishing a registry in partnership with its maritime trade associations, such as BIMCO and the ICS, that identifies vendors of software approved by the registry. Specific criteria have been put forward by regulators providing clarity to vessel owners and operators, carriers, and agents, producing bills of lading using technology under recommended providers that make the process seamless and effortless. The integrity of the original Bill of Lading in its original form cannot be compromised through technology inducements, putting the burden on industry to find a solution to such barriers that exist today in the willingness of nations to adopt the model law of the UK Act of 2023.

Vendors that are approved and vetted by registry managers need to ensure their decisions and vetting processes are not influenced by outside parties or hold biases toward individual investor groups that stand to profit from innovative technologies. Best practices require due diligence and a fiduciary duty on the part of vendor providers and the carriers, including their registry managers, experts, and regulators, to prevent acts of bribery, back-door deals, or hidden investors not named in the vendor qualifications.

The interoperability of the new system between different authorities is the largest struggle facing the industry and regulators in each country. The adoption of a new system requires large-scale international upgrades in areas of operating resources, documentation training, processes and procedures, human expertise, and removal of AI and autonomous solutions. This leads to state, national, and international consensus and collaboration through trade associations, federal government agencies, lawmakers, policy makers, and legal professionals, including the shippers, consumers, and end users of all cargo moved. Capital allocation by the top ten container liners in the world, who monopolize the market, with state-led subsidies, has already been executed in the adoption of online production of bills of lading and transmission of data under blockchain-type platforms.

In fact, container owners' announcement to move towards solely electronic forms by 2030 links their financial and operational commitment to a larger objective of digitalizing the whole marketplace under the great reset of 2030 of non-human connectivity for an increase in profits.

Other sectors that have adopted specific forms of E-Bills are the LNG carrier sectors, which have multiple transactions leading to the final delivery of the commodity across global jurisdictions. It will be interesting to see how LNG producers and exporters chartering LNG vessels under states such as Texas, Louisiana, Boston, New York, and Puerto Rico, from sourcing terminals, will integrate electronic bills of lading into their documentation departments and corporate policies.

The consumer will pay the increased fees for the new software systems, absorbing some benefit to its efficiency and timely delivery of goods under a paperless system, noting that maritime commissions need to ensure freight rates of foreign-flagged ships are monitored. This is another issue of legal contention that consumer advocates and shipper associations have been bringing forward in complaints to authorities such as the Federal Maritime Commission in the United States and its regulators, regarding unwarranted increases in freight rates. The recent increases by carriers in freight rates, specifically under carbon tax fees, clean fuel fees, and emissions credit schemes, are a prime example of burdening the end user and consumer with increased inflationary costs for the better good of the planet. The balance between both systems is not in line with the pace of technology and its pursuit of dominance in its innovation ambitions.

Today, we have three E-Bill systems, including newcomers into the market adopted by LNG carriers, container lines, and bulk carriers, known as BOLERO, ESS, and E-Title, being the most recent, noting others rely on existing ledger technology platforms. In its attempts to increase adoption of such systems in the shift to electronic form, the barriers remain, where all users need to sign up to a multi-party contract system that needs to be replicated. By contract, the law behind the bill of lading requires duplication of the original and copies, which requires compatibility by all users under the supply chain to make it seamless and efficient.[24]

This is at the heart of social, political, and economic considerations in moving a system forward with accountability and responsibility to the higher powers of decision makers globally. Additionally, those carriers who own the most cargo tonnage designated for the most lucrative trade lanes, specifically container carriers, customize their documentation to attain technological advancements through state funding.

Digitalization will drive a paperless workforce to a reduced labor force of document specialists, as robotization will perform these jobs, bringing harm and loss of jobs as a consequence. This is a consequence that today we have seen in the use of AI technology in the world of large data flows and blocks, in which human connectivity has been compromised in place of increased revenues, profits, and greed.

Presently, global tariffs and duties, specifically those imposed by the United States on the EU and other maritime nations such as China, have affected how cargo is routed, forcing leaders in the global shipping sectors to reroute their ships versus using vessels outside of their own nationality. A recent announcement by the leaders of the European Commission and their policy has made clear that rerouting ships is a better option than allowing US entry into the international commercial markets.

It is clear that investments will be made by maritime nations that create laws that support the transition because their country and industry will benefit them economically, politically, and socially, driven by profits. Blocking other nations from entering this lucrative business of digital technology of trade documents, specifically bills of lading, and control of document trading systems is the key objective of maritime-centered nation states, who have made it clear they will not buy ships made outside of their own country.

International agreements in the form of national state treaties are still seen to develop, noting that bilateral and multilateral agreements are developing between regions within a nation, specifically in Europe and Asia. The support arm of such agreements, politically not economically, is the international organizations supported under the UNECE and World Bank Sustainability programs of advanced developments driven by green, climate change, sustainability, and technology programs, with one common goal. Today, the UK and Singapore have acted on this common goal as far as to proclaim in the name of advancement, increased efforts to digitalize all trade systems under defined passports that they are proposing within their own states under a DDP program.

---

[24] Charlotte Winter, E-Bills of Lading, Global Publication, February 2018, Norton Rose Fulbright.com/en-US/knowledge/publications/b20094b6/e-bills-of-lading.

List Of Citations, References, And Additional Materials

1. Electronic Trade Documents Act 2023, Chapter 38, (UK).

2. Clifford Chance, UK Electronic Trade Documents Act 2023: A Further Step Towards Paperless Trade, August 2023, Blog Name, www.cliffordchance.com.

3. Hill Dickinson, UK's Electronic Trade Documentation Act now in force, October 13, 2023, https://www.hilldickinson.com/insights/articles/uks-electronic-trade-documents-act-now-force

4. Charlotte Winter, E-Bills of Lading, Global Publications, February 2018, Norton Rose Fulbright.com/en-US/knowledge/publications/b20094b6/ e-bills-of- lading.

5. DCSA Completes Standards-based Implementation, EBL transactions marking a major Industry milestone. May 15, 2025, https://www.dcsa.org/newsroom/ebl-interoperability-milestone.

Applicable Case Law And Arbitration Awards

Unicredit Bank AG v Euronav NV, (2022), EWHC 957 (Comm).

Arbitration Decisions.

1. 553 F. Supp. 2nd, 328 United States District Court, S.D. New York.

Padre Shipping, Inc., Plaintiff v. Yong He Shipping, Defendant.

2. 204 F. Supp. 2d 675 United States District Court, S.D. New York.

Central National - Gottesman, Inc. Plaintiff, v. M.V. Gertrude Oldendorff, her engines, boilers, etc. EO Oldenforff, Defendants.

RITA CONTE

Rita Conte led a documentation team in making software changes at a very turbulent time, specifically during the attacks of 9/11, when carriers around the world were faced with adopting new reporting requirements on all cargo entering and leaving foreign and domestic ports. She met this challenge through understanding what was required, in terms of relevant data on the ocean of bill of lading forms, acting as a subject specialist for the IT Vancouver team and their software provider, assuring technology systems did not compromise the legal information and integrity of the bill of lading. Responsible and successfully executing on all homeland and Canadian Border Security reporting internet interface requirements, she embraced and took the tasks to the next level, by acting as a liaison between the company's legal department in Bergen, Norway, and regulators, including law makers, in the US Department of Transportation, Homeland Security and the US Coast Guard. This included Canadian Transportation departments and Canadian Border Security Agencies, and the Canadian Coast Guard offices. Her ability to understand the legal, regulatory framework of trade documentation pertaining specifically to the transport bill of lading and its importance as a commercial contract of freight and transfer of goods allowed her to execute a new system successfully.

Rita's expertise resulted in the global fleet operating without delay, vessel arrest, or penalties for non-compliance, while assuring a new documentation export model of transparency, procedural clarity, and accuracy, met the needs of clients and authorities. Today, Rita continues to meet the needs of regulators, policy makers, insurance carriers, cargo owners, legal professionals, attorneys, shippers, cargo owners and consumers in providing expertise in dealing with issues relating to trade documentation.

Today, Rita is the person who can apply previous decision-making skills and expertise to today's changes in the electronic transmission of bills of lading successfully, while providing valuable experience and advice on how to manage this complex road.

Rita Conte

Trade and Transportation Policy, Regulatory Professional, Synergenics Consulting.

Email: rita@synergenicsconsulting.ca

Mobile no: 1-778-888-8065
Location: Vancouver, BC, Canada
Website:https://synergenicsconsulting.ca

**SYNERGENICS
CONSULTING**
Delivering Solutions